SUMMARY
&ANALYSIS

OF

Loonshots

HOW TO NURTURE THE CRAZY IDEAS THAT WIN WARS, CURE DISEASES, AND TRANSFORM INDUSTRIES

A GUIDE TO THE BOOK BY SAFI BAHCALL

TABLE OF CONTENTS

SYNOPSIS

In his book, *Loonshots: How to Nurture the Crazy Ideas That Win Wars, Cure Diseases, and Transform Industries*, Safi Bahcall introduces the concept of phase transitions and how loonshots can be nurtured to transform companies, industries, and entire nations. He defines a loonshot as an idea that is widely dismissed and ridiculed. This book is an attempt to convince mankind to embrace radical ideas that have the potential of making our lives better, no matter how crazy they may sound.

The book is divided into three parts. In part one, Bahcall highlights several people who attempted loonshots and succeeded. He mentions notable characters such as Steve Jobs, Edwin Land, and Juan Trippe, who generated loonshots that revolutionized their respective industries. However, some of these innovators fell into a trap that ultimately bankrupted their companies. Bahcall explains how organizations can avoid this trap and keep generating new ideas.

In part two of the book, Bahcall discusses the science behind phase transitions and the importance of understanding sudden changes in group behavior. He provides a technique that can help predict the point at which a company will transition from embracing loonshots to rejecting them. With this kind of knowledge, it is possible to predict when wildfires, traffic jams, and even terrorist attacks will occur. The final part of the book is an analysis of how loonshot ideas have influenced world history and the impact this has had on modern society.

PART I: ENGINEERS OF SERENDIPITY

CHAPTER ONE

Bahcall opens the book by describing how the Allies managed to defeat the Nazis in WWII. Nazi Germany was far more advanced in terms of technological capability, but when Vannevar Bush created a new system for developing breakthroughs, the tide shifted dramatically. His solution was to create phase separation and dynamic equilibrium between the old and new systems.

Key Takeaway: When fighting a war, it's the ability to embrace innovation that leads to victory.

According to Bahcall, one of the first things that Vannevar Bush learned as a volunteer military scientist was how not to fight a war. During WWI, Bush had a novel idea to create a magnetic device that could detect submarines. However, the Navy rejected the idea and the armed services continued to slash funding for new technological research. At that point, Bush discovered that supplying new ideas was not the solution to winning a war. The key was to get the military officers to accept these radical ideas and use them on the battlefield, something that was extremely difficult considering their perception of civilian scientists as lesser beings. Both the military and scientists had to trust and respect one another and embrace their different skills to win the war.

Key Takeaway: Under certain special conditions, two phases of an organization can coexist.

One of the problems that the US military faced prior to WWII was that its generals tended to recycle their tactics and weapons. While Germany was utilizing science to create advanced weaponry, the US was manufacturing more planes, guns, and ships. Bahcall refers to this as the *franchise phase*—doing more of the same. To defeat the Nazis, it was important to adopt a new phase—the *loonshot phase*. A loonshot is an idea that is so crazy that most people ridicule and denounce it. Under normal conditions, it is impossible to merge these two phases. But 1938 was not an ordinary condition. The US military needed the tried-and-tested way of building munitions and troops as well as embrace radically new technologies. The key was to create a new structure based on both phases, rather than change the military culture.

Key Takeaway: To nurture new ideas, separate the franchise phase from the loonshot phase.

The first rule of creating a structure that will nurture loonshots is the separation of phases. When you have an organization that comprises "artists" (radical thinkers) and "soldiers" (status-quo employees), you must keep these two groups separated. The radical thinkers are responsible for coming up with high-risk ideas that the soldiers are likely to quickly dismiss. If you do not cocoon the artists and protect their early-stage ideas, they will be vilified and shut down by the soldier group. This is what happens in the military and major corporations. Creating phase separation requires developing separate systems for both phases and also physically separating the creative team from the rigid group.

Key Takeaway: Provide equal support for both the loonshot artists and franchise soldiers.

To maintain dynamic equilibrium in an organization, you must equally love and respect both the franchise soldiers and loonshot artists. During his first stint as Apple CEO, Steve Jobs openly favored the nerdy artists and belittled the suit-wearing soldiers in the company. As a result of continued hostility between the two groups, the Mac launch failed commercially, Apple suffered financially, and Jobs was fired. Bahcall argues that there must be an open transfer of ideas, constant feedback, and support from top management in order to get the franchise and loonshot groups to successfully work together.

CHAPTER TWO

Every idea that changed the world was rejected at the first hurdle. Bahcall argues that loonshots must go through at least three deaths, or three failures, before they are considered worthy of deeper consideration. This is what happened to Akiro Endo, the Japanese scientist who first discovered that a fungal extract can be used to lower cholesterol and prevent heart attacks and strokes. Endo spent 16 years struggling to get his statin drug approved, but whenever he achieved a breakthrough, something always went awry. But he never gave up, and despite the fact that Merck (an American drug manufacturer) later took the credit for it, Endo's loonshot was ultimately validated. The secret, therefore, is to keep innovating rather than giving up your crazy idea. You must nurture and protect your fragile loonshot.

Key Takeaway: False fails are the biggest killers of loonshots.

Though every loonshot must go through at least three massive failures before it eventually succeeds, some fails are more common than others. According to Bahcall, the most common factor that halts a new idea is the False Fail. This is a mistake that is usually linked to the loonshot but is actually a result of flawed testing. For example, when Akiro Endo tested his statin drug on rats, it failed. What he didn't realize is that rats don't have bad cholesterol, thus the drug wouldn't show the right results. In his second fail, the results showed that his statin drug causes cancer in dogs. Again, it was later discovered that the test results were severely flawed. After each fail, use of the drug was ceased, but Endo kept pursuing his research until he proved that the fails were not credible.

Key Takeaway: Every loonshot needs a project champion.

Most people credit the creator of an idea or product but few realize the role that the project champion plays. Endo was a rare case because he was the inventor *and* champion of his own project. That is why after he left the company, nobody bothered to investigate the False Fails. If there had been another individual to act as project champion, Endo's program would have been revived. According to Bahcall, US military records do not mention the person who championed the invention of radar. From the outset, the project scientists faced intense resistance from military generals and they eventually lost hope and gave up. But when Admiral Parsons joined the Naval Research Lab, he instantly saw the potential of radar and harassed top military brass until they finally agreed to fund the radar project. The best companies separate the roles of inventor and champion because the champion can promote while the inventor creates.

Key Takeaway: Instead of dismissing criticism, investigate your failure with an open mind.

Whenever a new idea is proposed, there is always resistance. When the idea fails, the ridicule gets worse. As the creator, you can easily be tempted to defend your idea. However, this approach is wrong. Bahcall suggests that you do what Endo and Thiel, did: ask yourself *why* the failure occurred. Endo experimented further and discovered where the problem was. Peter Thiel wanted to invest in Facebook but was told that social networks were a fad and users were abandoning social media websites in droves. But upon digging deeper into the data, Thiel discovered that users were leaving because the interface was not friendly—not because social networks were unpopular. Instead of lashing out at critics, you should quietly investigate and learn why your idea isn't working.

CHAPTER THREE

Bahcall describes the third rule that governs loonshots: the need to differentiate between the two types of loonshots. He refers to them as the *P-Type* and *S-Type* of loonshot. If an organization focuses too much on one type of loonshot and misses out on the other, the failure can be fatal.

Key Takeaway: P-type and S-type loonshots have very different characteristics.

Bahcall defines a P-type loonshot as a surprising innovation in a product. This occurs when someone invents a new product and the world dismisses it as unworkable or undesirable to the market. This is what happened when Bell Telephone Company started out. Nobody believed that the market would embrace something called a telephone, and investors mockingly referred to the product as a toy. Yet at its peak, Bell was more valuable than Microsoft, GE, and Apple, at their peaks, combined. When a P-type loonshot comes into the market, competitors normally die off quickly and dramatically. Netflix and Amazon came in with streaming videos and quickly killed off the video rental company, Blockbuster.

S-type loonshots are those that introduce an innovative strategy. This can be a new way of doing something or a new way of applying an existing product. For example, when Sam Walton decided to locate his stores outside the major cities, the business world said that there's no way his strategy could be profitable. Yet Walmart managed to deliver existing products for cheaper, ultimately knocking out retail behemoths such as Gibson's, Woolworths, and Ames. S-type loonshots tend to kill off competitors more gradually because nobody really sees them coming, and few really understand why they work. This is why it took 30 years for Walmart to establish itself as the most dominant retailer.

Key Takeaway: It is better to master and nurture the S-type loonshot.

According to Bahcall, S-type loonshots are complex because they are based on consumer and market behavior. Therefore, it's not easy to predict their outcome. One rare event is enough to turn an S-type loonshot into a success. Nobody foresaw the deregulation of the US airline industry in 1978. All of a sudden, new airlines sprang up with new strategies, such as frequent flier programs and computerized reservations. Though these changes in strategy were minor and non-glamorous, they led to the demise of Pan Am, which had reigned for decades as the largest airline in the world.

Juan Trippe, Pan Am CEO, was a master at P-type loonshots—jumbo planes and jet engines. However, Bob Crandall, CEO of American Airlines, mastered S-type loonshots. After deregulation, the only airline that stayed profitable was American Airlines. If you want to avoid being blindsided by sudden shocks to the industry, you are better off learning how to nurture S-type loonshots.

Key Takeaway: Focusing on P-type loonshots instead of strategy will leave you blindsided.

Bahcall argues that almost every organization that has a P-type leader is eventually blindsided. IBM dominated the computer hardware industry in the 1980s and 90s, but it failed to recognize a shift in consumer behavior. Customers cared more about software that they did about hardware. Ultimately, Intel and Microsoft software drove IBM out of business. IBM may have hit the P-type loonshot, but it missed the strategy needed to stay dominant. Bahcall calls this the *Moses Trap*, where a leader of an organization stays at the top of the mountain for so long (anointing P-type loonshots) that they fail to communicate with their soldiers and creatives on the ground.

CHAPTER FOUR

Edwin Land is known for his audacious inventions in the field of photography, video, and imaging. He is credited with inventing the Polaroid camera, the first digital film machine, as well as helping the US military design U2 spy planes that could take photos of Russian assets all over the world. However, Land is also known for colossal oversights that led to the demise of the Polaroid Company. Despite being a genius who was extremely capable of launching P-type loonshots, he still fell into the Moses Trap that seems to dog many innovators.

Bahcall defines the Moses Trap as a situation where ideas only advance if the leader says so, and this leader obsesses over loonshots rather than focusing on an effective strategy. As CEOs, they continue to judge new ideas instead of allowing the creatives to do their job. He mentions Edwin Land, Juan Trippe, and Steve Jobs as examples of visionaries who successfully achieved phase separation but failed to ensure a dynamic equilibrium. Thus they built great companies but still got caught in a Moses Trap.

Key Takeaway: The Moses Trap always follows a predictable three-step pattern.

Step One – The new products propel the company forward as the franchise brings in more revenue. Since the leader prefers P-type loonshots, the company uses the income to generate more P-type loonshots. Trippe created new engines and Pan Am began to fly faster and farther.

Land invented instant photos and his Polaroid Company churned out instant color cameras.

Step Two – The leader is blinded by the success of their P-type loonshots. Trippe saw how other airlines were coming up with new strategies, but he ignored the competition. Land knew the potential of digital film but stuck with his instant film because he was making more money from instant-print film cartridges. Digital doesn't need film, so Land dismissed it as unprofitable. In both cases, the leaders excessively relied on their strengths and left their blind side open.

Step Three – Moses attains total control and rules by decree. Instead of Land acting like the chairman and letting appointing a research director, he decided he wanted to play both roles. He ended up usurping the powers of his research groups and overruled them at every turn. This is what killed the Polavision instant-movie camera right after its launch.

CHAPTER FIVE

In this chapter, Bahcall describes how a leader can avoid falling into the Moses Trap by creating a balance between the franchise group and the creative loonshot group. He describes in detail how Steve jobs failed to do this during his first stint as Apple CEO. But after experiencing massive failures and successes working with NeXT and Pixar, Jobs matured enough to understand the importance of creating a dynamic equilibrium in a company. According to Bahcall, escaping the Moses Trap requires you to distinguish between two specific leadership mindsets.

Key Takeaway: Teams must go beyond an outcomes mindset and adopt a systems mindset.

There are two types of mindsets that a team can adopt—an outcome mindset and a systems mindset. An outcome mindset is where a team undertakes a project, it fails, and the team tries to identify *why* the project/product failed. Bahcall also refers to this as Level 1 strategy. If you made an investment that reaped a loss, you can evaluate why that outcome occurred. The problem with teams that have an outcome mindset is that they don't dig deep enough, so they only commit to working harder when they fail. When they succeed, they assume they are geniuses, move on, and end up failing down the road.

A systems mindset is where the team goes deeper and tries to find out the decisions that led to failure. This is also referred to as Level 2 strategy. If you made an investment that failed, you can analyze the decision-making process that led you to invest in that company. Did you do your due diligence? Were you distracted? How can you change your financial analysis strategy to avoid repeating the mistake? Teams with this kind of mindset tend to succeed over the long term because they probe and learn from both their wins as well as their losses. If they made a bad decision, got lucky, and reaped a positive result, digging deeper will reveal this fact. Thus they will change their decision process.

Key Takeaway: The PARC Trap is the opposite of the Moses Trap.

According to Bahcall, PARC (Xerox's Palo Alto Research Center) represents the inverse of the dreaded Moses Trap. PARC is credited with inventing the first of many devices: PCs with graphics capability, laser printers, word processors, and Ethernet. But Xerox never commercialized any of these products because the franchise group decided to shoot down every innovation that the loonshot group came up with. Unlike the Moses Trap where the leader over-controls the launch of loonshots, the PARC Trap practically squashes every single loonshot that tries to emerge from within the company.

PART II: THE SCIENCE OF SUDDEN CHANGE

CHAPTER SIX

Bahcall defines a phase transition as a sudden transformation in behavior caused by gradual shifts. For example, a traffic jam isn't usually caused by an accident or a stalled vehicle. When the driver ahead of you steps on the brakes, you are also forced to stop within seconds. However, it takes you longer than a few seconds to get back to cruising speed. The car behind you will take twice as long as you to cruise at their original speed, and so forth with the cars behind them. These minor decelerations are responsible for causing major disruptions in traffic flow. Therefore, a phase transition is the result of two opposing forces that create an imbalance in the system.

Key Takeaway: A system is defined by its entropic and binding energy.

When men are single, they tend to fall under the control of two competing forces entropy and binding energy. Younger single men use most of their energy chasing wealth and fame, and thus they are *controlled by entropy*. Older single men have already achieved financial stability, so they are seeking to settle down and start a family. Thus they are controlled by *binding energy*. Entropy creates movement and vigor while binding energy creates stability.

Key Takeaway: To prevent a system from snapping, we must identify the control parameters.

Bahcall defines a control parameter as a property that you can slowly alter to stimulate a phase transition. If you place marbles in an egg carton, each marble will rest quietly in its egg well. But if you begin to shake the egg carton, the marbles will begin to vibrate. The more energy you put into shaking the carton, the more the marbles will move. Past a certain threshold, some of them will end up flying into the neighboring egg wells. In this case, you have stimulated a phase transition, and the control parameter is the strength of your shaking.

However, there is more than one control parameter in this system. If the egg wells are 100 times deeper, then the binding energy will be much stronger than before. Therefore, binding energy is also a control parameter. By knowing the number of control parameters in a system, it becomes easier to determine and manage the point at which the system will snap. This is how it's possible to know when a forest fire will erupt, a traffic jam will occur, or a terror attack is imminent.

Key Takeaway: Phase transition models can be used to identify and stop online terror cells.

According to Bahcall, stopping a terror attack is possible if you focus on how terror cells transition. Percolation-style models can be used to examine terror cell clusters rather than monitoring the behavior of individuals. Secondly, there are mathematical techniques that can be used to identify those clusters that have the greatest influence. The third strategy of fighting terrorists is to fragment large clusters into smaller ones so that they do not transition to the next phase—an attack.

CHAPTER SEVEN

Bahcall uses the concept of phase transitions to explain why the size of a company directly influences whether it accepts loonshots or focuses on franchises. Small groups usually focus on collective goals and loonshots. As the company grows, more emphasis is instead channeled toward individual career goals. But at some point, the company grows so big that loonshots don't stand a chance. People begin to gravitate toward ideas that are less risky to preserve the status quo. In this chapter, Bahcall shows how to control this transition and prevent it from happening.

Key Takeaway: 150 is the optimal number for human groupings.

In the 1800s, the Mormons were facing intense persecution from other settlers in areas such as Missouri and Illinois. Faced with death threats and forced expulsion, Brigham Young told his fellow Mormons to organize themselves into companies of 150 and head west. A hundred years later, after studying monkeys, a researcher called Robin Dunbar theorized that the optimal size of a social group is 150. Soon enough, the idea went viral and organizations and social networks began using "Dunbar's Number" as the standard for bringing teams, students, and online friends together. Though some experts disagree with the idea of extrapolating human behavior from monkeys, Bahcall believes that there is some truth to this observation. Something definitely changes when a group crosses a specific size threshold.

Key Takeaway: Three design parameters can be used to predict employee decisions.

Bahcall states that in an organization, employees are motivated by three design parameters: base salary, management span, and equity fraction. An employee can either spend their time working on a project or schmoozing with the boss to get a promotion. For example, being promoted in a large organization may come with a 200 percent salary bump. Therefore, schmoozing would be a great way to spend your time. However, if being promoted only gets you a two percent salary increase, then you are better off working on your project. This is more likely in a smaller company.

The next factor is management span. If there are 100 fellow employees under every supervisor, competing for the boss's attention may be difficult. Therefore, politicking may be a waste of time. However, if there are only two of you under one supervisor, then you will spend more time politicking to get that promotion. Equity fraction refers to how much you are paid based on work quality. If you are good at your job, and the company makes more money because of it, you will choose to work rather than politicking.

Key Takeaway: Two other fitness parameters influence employee behavior.

Apart from design parameters, an employee's decisions may be influenced by two subtle incentives. These are project-skill fit and return-on-politics. If you are incredibly skilled at your job, then you don't have to politick because your work will always speak for you. But if you not as skilled, you know that lobbying is the only way to get ahead in the company. Return-on-politics refers to how much weight politics has when promotions are made. If the managers enjoy politicking, they will promote people who play office politics; and vice versa.

Therefore, to determine the critical size of a company that will favor loonshots over politics, you must combine all five factors together in an equation.

CHAPTER EIGHT

In this chapter, Bahcall explains how to raise the Magic Number—150—so that an organization can successfully generate and launch loonshots. The goal is to eliminate politics and get people to focus on their projects. He proposes six strategies that include structural changes within the organization, hiring the right people, and using the right incentives.

Key Takeaway: To enhance radical innovation, reduce the level of politicking.

Many organizational structures are designed in a way that encourage employees to climb the career ladder and get a bigger office and salary. However, this also creates internal rivalries, which can kill off loonshots. DARPA (Defense Advanced Research Program Agency) is able to nurture and launch numerous loonshots because it is designed to mimic a group of small startups. The research teams have free reign to come up with innovative ideas because there is no career ladder. Therefore, politicking is a waste of time.

Key Takeaway: The career ladder should be replaced with soft equity.

Once an organization has eliminated tangible, hard equity incentives such as a bigger salary, they must find another way to motivate employees. One strategy is soft equity, which refers to an intangible motivating force. Successful project managers are given public recognition by peers, allowed to choose their preferred projects, negotiate contracts, and control their schedules. A company can also decide to hire an external auditor to evaluate a candidate for promotion. This eliminates the need for employees to engage in internal politics.

Key Takeaway: Increasing project-skill fit can incentivize employees to achieve more.

Project-skill fit means the employee has the required skills to succeed at a project. If an employee isn't adding any value to a team, it may be because they don't have enough skills. However, it may also be possible that they do have skills but they have been assigned to the wrong project (undermatch). Another scenario is that some employees may be too skilled that they quickly get bored by projects way below their competence level (overmatch). Bahcall suggests that managers must dedicate time to matching employees to roles that stretch them enough without overwhelming them.

Key Takeaway: High wage dispersion reduces the motivation of mid-level employees.

In an organization where top-level executives are incentivized using hard equity and low-level employees get very little in terms of bonuses, it's the mid-level workers who suffer the most. The employees at the bottom are easily evaluated based on how well they oversee one product or service. The senior managers are evaluated based on how well they maintain stability and quench disruptive turf wars below them. But the employees in the middle have to juggle many products and services while trying to survive the backstabbing from fellow mid-level managers. They all want to rise to the top and enjoy what the senior managers are getting. Therefore, they are more likely to focus on promotions rather than project success. The solution is to reward employees based on results rather than rank.

Key Takeaway: A wide management span nurtures loonshots more than a narrow one.

According to Bahcall, fine-tuning the management span is one way that a company can launch more audacious ideas. With a narrow management span (manager supervising five or fewer employees), a group has tighter controls and fewer failures. Unfortunately, this means fewer loonshots are nurtured. With a wider management span (supervising 15 or more employees), there are fewer controls, more experiments, greater independence, and more failures. This is more likely to nurture loonshots.

PART III: THE MOTHER OF ALL LOONSHOTS

CHAPTER NINE

Bahcall states that the mother of all loonshots was the development of the scientific method. He explains how industries and nations can create loonshot nurseries and why China and India were overrun by European colonial power despite being the pioneers of the industrial revolution. Ultimately, those nations that seek to avoid slipping into obscurity must understand that ignoring loonshots can prove catastrophic.

Key Takeaway: There are three conditions that enable a loonshot nursery to flourish.

History shows that sometimes companies, industries or nations can exist under similar conditions yet some encourage loonshots while others do not. According to Bahcall, three conditions are responsible for this phenomenon:

- Phase separation

- Dynamic equilibrium

- Critical mass

Key Takeaway: Different companies in the same industry can partner to nurture loonshots.

In the early 1900s, Hollywood was dominated by the major studios—Columbia, Paramount, Warner Brothers, etc. They controlled both movie production as well as theater houses. But in 1948, the US government broke up the oligopoly and studios could no longer own theaters. This created two markets—major studios that focus on franchises and smaller production companies that focus on loonshot projects. When a small studio produces a film, they sell the marketing rights to a larger one. This dynamic equilibrium ensures that the industry churns out innovative films like *Slumdog Millionaire* while maintaining the stability that comes with franchises like *Iron Man*.

Key Takeaway: Critical mass is the spark that ignites a loonshot.

To ignite a loonshot, you must ensure that there are enough committed people in the loonshot group. Commitment is usually in the form of providing adequate funding and attracting the best talent. To elaborate on this concept, Bahcall compares Boston to Detroit. Though both cities have biotech firms, it is Boston that is known as a biotech hub because there are over 200 such companies in the city. Detroit only has a handful. As a result, most venture capitalists and biomedical firms have moved to Boston, and this has created an environment where new ideas thrive. The money and top talent are readily available.

Key Takeaway: England became a powerhouse because it nurtured the first loonshot nursery.

For centuries, it has been a well-known fact that China and India were the birthplaces of great scientific and mathematical thinkers. However, many of the inventions and theories of modern science are linked to England. According to Bahcall, England overtook everyone, including fellow European nations, because it had the first successful loonshot nursery to be established within one country. All the men who are considered the fathers of modern science passed through the Royal Society of London. Isaac Newton, Robert Hooke, Robert Boyle, and many others were able to invent freely and exchange ideas thanks to the loonshot nursery that was the Royal Society of London.

EDITORIAL REVIEW

Loonshots is one of those books that remind us that most of the technologies we enjoy today are the creations of individuals who were considered nuts. Yet they believed in their ideas enough to make them a reality. Safi Bahcall has managed to combine science, technology, history, and business into a thought-provoking book that is a must-read for every leader.

In this book, Bahcall poses three major arguments. The first is that the biggest breakthroughs are the result of ideas that are so out-of-this-world that the individual who comes up with them is considered unhinged. Due to the skepticism and ridicule, most loonshots never see the light of day.

His second argument is that you must have a large enough team to convert a loonshot into an accepted technology. However, contrary to popular opinion, it's the structure of the team that determines success rather than the organizational culture.

Finally, Bahcall argues that phase transitions are the key to nurturing loonshots. Phase transitions refer to sudden shifts from one behavior to another, like water shifting from liquid to ice. By understanding the phases that a project team goes through, we can understand how to control these transitions to ensure loonshots are continually nurtured.

So how does the concept of phase transitions work? In a startup company, every employee holds a high stake in the success of a project. If a loonshot project succeeds, everybody gains, but if it fails, everyone suffers. The issue of rank doesn't matter as much as the stakes involved. Therefore, employees focus on audacious ideas that will guarantee their survival. However, as the company grows larger, rank and job titles take priority. The guys at the top enjoy bigger perks and therefore, they will do anything to preserve these perks. They will shut down any crazy project that threatens their fat bonuses. Therefore, the goal is to foresee when this transition will occur and stop it.

Another interesting element is the separation of the artists (creative, loonshot group) from the soldiers (franchise group that prefers the status quo). If you do not create a buffer between these two groups, the soldiers will block the loonshots. There has to be a dynamic equilibrium so that both groups share feedback. Not all loonshots will work in real life, so the artists need to be told why, what, and where to make changes. The career ladder and politicking must be eliminated. Employees who spend time schmoozing to get ahead won't have time for generating innovative ideas.

The book is an insightful lesson in history. Bahcall provides intricate details of behind-the-scenes machinations that defined the world as we know it. Some would argue that Bahcall spends more time on historical anecdotes and very little in terms of key takeaways. You may have to wait until the end of a chapter to find the key takeaways he is trying to highlight.

At the core of it all, the idea is that breakthrough ideas usually fail multiple times before they succeed. It is genius meeting serendipity. This should encourage anyone out there who is loony enough to take that bold, but innovative risk you've been waiting for.

BACKGROUND ON AUTHOR

Safi Bahcall is a biotech entrepreneur and physicist who co-founded his own biotechnology company, Synta Pharmaceuticals Corp., in 2001 The company is involved in research and development of new cancer drugs. He served as its CEO for 13 years.

He was born in Princeton, New Jersey in 1968 to parents who were astrophysicists. Bahcall began studying mathematics and physics at Princeton University from the age of 13. He then attended Harvard and graduated *summa cum laude* in 1988 with a B.A. in Physics. He later went to Stanford University and graduated in 1995 with a Ph.D. in Theoretical Physics before completing his post-doctoral degree at University of California, Berkeley.

In 1998, he joined McKinsey & Company as a consultant and worked for three years before leaving to start his own firm. In 2008, he was awarded the Ernst & Young award for New England Biotechnology Entrepreneur of the Year. Bahcall was appointed to President Obama's Council of Advisors on Science and Technology and served between 2011 and 2012.

Though *Loonshots* is his first book, it has been selected as one of the top 10 leadership and business books of 2019.by the *Washington Post*, *Inc. Magazine*, and *Business Insider*. Bahcall and his wife Magda have two kids. They live in Cambridge, Massachusetts

★★★*END OF BOOK SUMMARY*★★★

If you enjoyed this ZIP Reads publication, we encourage you to purchase a copy of <u>the original book.</u>

We'd also love an honest review on Amazon.com!

Want **FREE** book summaries delivered weekly? Sign up for our email list and get notified of all our new releases, free promos, and $0.99 deals!

No spam, just books.

Sign up at <u>www.zipreads.co</u>

Made in the USA
Lexington, KY
04 July 2019